as I watch you Grow things I want you to Know

Letters to my Son

with love always

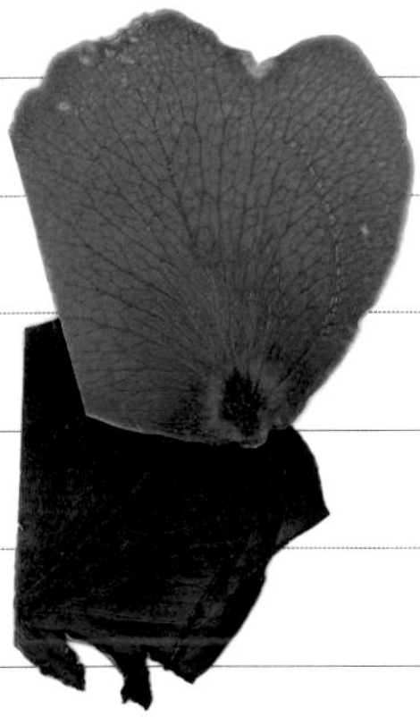

Made in the USA
San Bernardino, CA
17 February 2020

64590856R00058